FUNKY

CHICKENS

BENJAMIN ZEPHANIAH

FUNKY

CHICKENS

PUFFIN BOOKS

PUFFIN BOOKS

Published by the Penguin Group
Penguin Books Ltd, 80 Strand, London WC2R 0RL, England
Penguin Putnam Inc., 375 Hudson Street, New York, New York 10014, USA
Penguin Books Australia Ltd, 250 Camberwell Road, Camberwell, Victoria 3124, Australia
Penguin Books Canada Ltd, 10 Alcorn Avenue, Toronto, Ontario, Canada M4V 3B2
Penguin Books India (P) Ltd, 11 Community Centre, Panchsheel Park, New Delhi – 110 017, India
Penguin Books (NZ) Ltd, Cnr Rosedale and Airborne Roads, Albany, Auckland, New Zealand
Penguin Books (South Africa) (Pty) Ltd, 24 Sturdee Avenue, Rosebank 2196, South Africa

Penguin Books Ltd, Registered Offices: 80 Strand, London WC2R 0RL, England

www.penguin.com

First published by Viking 1996
Published in Puffin Books 1997
21

Text copyright © Benjamin Zephaniah, 1996
Illustrations copyright © The Point, 1996
All rights reserved

The moral right of the author (and illustrator) has been asserted

Filmset in Sabon and Franklin Gothic

Made and printed in England by Clays Ltd, St Ives plc

British Library Cataloguing in Publication Data
A CIP catalogue record for this book is available from the British Library

www.greenpenguin.co.uk

Penguin Books is committed to a sustainable future
for our business, our readers and our planet.
The book in your hands is made from paper
certified by the Forest Stewardship Council.

To the memory of Danny the Cat _____

_____ A great source of inspiration and a brilliant footballer.

CONTENTS

NATURAL ANTHEM

✝ **God** save our gracious green
Long live our glorious scene
God save our green.

✝ **Dis** ting is serious
Do it for all of us
Save our asparagus,
God save
Our
Green.

HEALTH FOOD STOP

Little Miss Muffet
Sat on her tuffet
Eating her organic pears,
Along came a spider
Disguised as her driver
To nibble her carob éclairs.

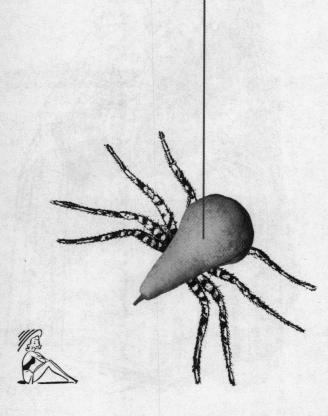

YORK'S SCHOOL REPORT

✗ **The** Grand Old Duke of York
He could not count to **ten**,
When he got to **four** and a half
He had to start again,
On exam day he started at **none**
And he slowly progressed to **one**,
By the time he got **two**, **three** and **four**
His memory had gone.

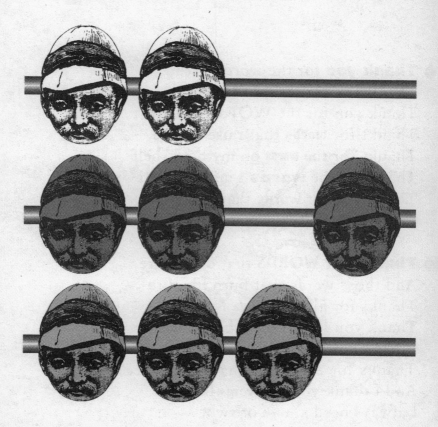

FOR WORD

Thank you for the *words* I read
Thank you for the **words** I need
Thank you for the WORDS so great
Thanks for **words** that raise debate,
Thanks for the **words** on my bookshelf
Thanx for the **words** I make myself
Thank you for **words** that make me cry
And words that leave me feeling dry.

Thanks for WORDS that do inspire
And those words that burn like fire
Thanks for all the *words* I note
Thank you for all the *words* I quote,
I thank you for the **words** like me
Thanks for *WORDS* that set me free
And I thank you for *words* like you
I always need a word or two.

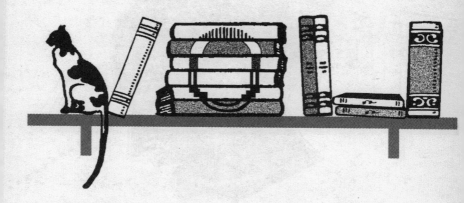

Thanks for **words** that make things plain
And words that help me to explain
Thanks for **words** that make life fun
And *words* that help me overcome,
Thanks for **words** that make me rap
Thanks for *words* that make me clap
Thanks for WORDS that make me smile
Thanks for WORDS with grace and style.

Thanks for all those **words** that sing
Thanks for **words** are everything
Thanks for all the **WORDS** like this
And little sloppy *words* like kiss,
Thanks for **words** like hip-hooray
And those cool **words** I like to say
Thanks for *words* that reach and touch
Thank you very, very much.

LIBRARY OLOGY

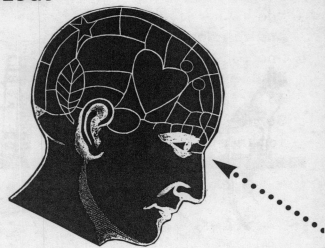

⑤ I have a date with Su Ling Lee
We're meeting at the library
At 5 o'clock by history
I'll show her some myth*ology*,
And if we have the energy
We'll check out some the*ology*
And if there is good chemistry
We'll dance by music*ology*.

➤ We'll sail through ocean*ology*
And get some cool lith*ology*
And roundabout psych*ology*
I'll sweet talk her top*ology*,
With science and techn*ology*
We'll have some soci*ology*
And touch each others botany
With organic homoe*opathy*.

★ She knows so much cosmology
I do luv her ecology
And reading her astrology
I note she has anatomy,
I'll use my best phraseology
To get her to phonology
So we can lexicology
Together in the library.

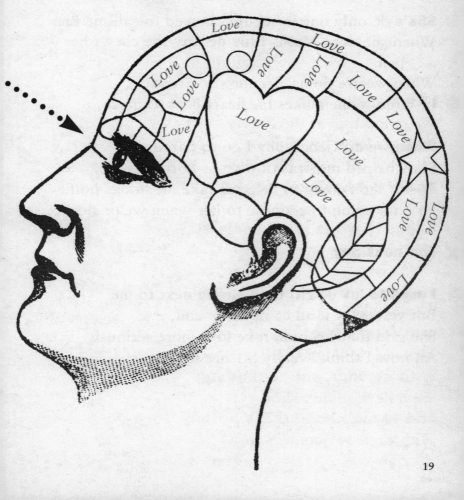

SERIOUS LUV

✔ Monday Morning

I really luv de girl dat's sitting next to me
I think she thinks like me an she's so cool,
I think dat we could live for ever happily
I want to marry her when I leave school.

She's de only one in school allowed to call me Ben
When she does Maths I luv de way she chews her
     pen,
When we are doing Art she's so artistic
In Biology she makes me heart beat so quick.

When we do Geography I go to paradise
She's helped me draw a map of Borneo twice!
Today she's going to help me take me books home
So I am going to propose to her when we're alone.

✗ The next day

I used to luv de girl dat's sitting next to me
But yesterday it all came to an end,
She said that I should take love more seriously
An now I think I really luv her friend.

JELLYVISION

☆ **Daddy's** on de telly
Showing off his belly
He wants to be a star
But he's not getting far,
He tried to read de weather
He really did endeavour
But he's really not dat clever
He made no sense whatsoever.

◯ **Daddy's** on de box
Squeezing all his spots
He wants to read de news
But he only knows de blues,
He's tried to do a trick
Wid a rabbit an a stick
But de rabbit waz too slick
An me Daddy's not too quick.

❧ **I know you don't believe me**
But Daddy's on de TV
He's doing a commercial
Dat's very controversial,
He's trying to sell hair spray
Dat stops hair going grey
Which haz extra dirty clay
They should lock Daddy away.

✗ **Daddy** did not get permission
To go on de television
He thinks life will be easier
Working in de media,
But I don't think he's ready
He just does not look steady
He's shivering like jelly
Standing on de telly.

THE BUSKER

She strums upon the guitar
Like a rainbow strums the sky,
Her fingers sing a song
Upon the strings,
She brings to me old memories
Of a reggae lullaby,
And all the histories
That good reggae brings.

As I receive fine tuning
My hard times drift away,
My income tax bills
Weigh me down no more,
East Ham is full of fountains
Vibrations have their say
And all my ills receive
An instant cure.

Her music making makes me
A very gentle man
The melody is making
Common sense,
The passers by are busy
Making millions
And all I have to give
Is twenty pence.

BIRTHRIGHTS

☆ **Baby** *is* a SUPERSTAR
She really **luvs** de stage
She's **HOT**
She's *cool*
Yu **cannot** guess her age,
Baby *is* a SUPERSTAR
Don't tell *her* wot to do
She's **safe**
She's GREAT
She's very much *like you.*
Baby *is* a SUPERSTAR
So tek a picture *quick*
She *shines*
She's fine
So very *poetic,*
Baby *is* a SUPERSTAR
She **sings**, she **plays**, she *writes*
Let's **listen** to her freedom songs
She's in *concert* tonight.

I DE RAP GUY

I am de rapping rasta
I rap de lyrics fasta
Dan a Ford Cortina
Or a double ghetto blasta,
When royals are listening
They proclaim me as a king
I am way out an travelling
Not a puppet on a string.

I am de rapping rasta
De lyrical masta
Dey say I am good to go
So I go wid de flow,
If yu really want to know
Yu should book me for a show
I will tek yu high an low
Like an eagle or a roe.

What I spread is unity
Or to put it simply
I want racial harmony
In de world community,
I am big an I am bad
So bad I will mek yu glad
An you'll hav to tell ya Dad
Bout de rapper yu just had.

I rap on de move
Wid a little tongue an groove
Wid ability to soothe
Warmongers may not approve,
I can put yu in your place
Wid a little drum an bass
I am proud of every race
I out ran de steeplechase.

I am de rapping rasta
Flesh an bone not plaster
My ideas are very green
An I keep me rapping clean,
Let me take you on a tour
I know what I'm rapping for,
I can rap from coast to coast
An I don't like to brag or boast.

IF YU SEE

+ If yu see a zebra crossing
Stop an let it cross
If yu see a flower flowing
Let it flow,
If yu see someone who's bossy
Tell dem who's boss,
If yu see someone wid knowledge
Let dem know.

IF YU HEAR

● **If** yu hear some Rock an Roll
Try to rock an roll
If yu hear a rumour spreading
Mek sum room,
If yu hear a mole
Trying to dig a hole
Yu hav heard
A very dirty little tune.

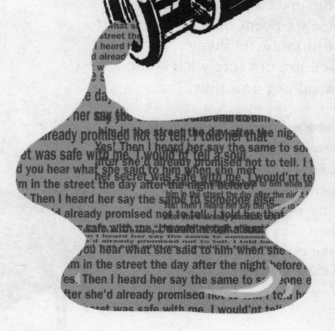

POETICS

There's a poem on your face
There's a poem in the sky
There's a poem in outta space
There are poems passing by,
There are poems in your dreams
There are poems in your head
Sometimes I cannot get to sleep
Cause there are poems in me bed.

There are poems in me tea
There are poems on me toast
I have found much poetry
In the place I love the most,
There's a poem right in front of you
Get to know its rhyme,
If you are not sure what to do
Just call it poem time.

There's a poem in me shoes
There's a poem in me shirt
When the poem meets the blues
It can really, really hurt,
Other poems make you grin
When they dribble off your chin
Some poems think they are great
So they like to make you ...

Wait

I see poems in your teeth
I see poems in me cat
I hear poems underneath
Going rata tat tat tat,
This one has not finished yet
It keeps coming on the beat
It is soggy and it's wet
But it's also very sweet.

There are poems for the **ear** ✚
There are poems for the page
Some poems are not quite clear
But they get better with age,
There are poems for the hip
There are poems for the hop
Everything is poetic
Poetry will never stop.

There are poems on your **fingers** ☞
There's a poem on your nose
If you give it time to linger
It will grow and grow and grow,
There's a poem in you beautiful
Can't you see it
It's right

There, ★
I think it's so incredible
There are poems
Everywhere.

31

EPIC

 My favourite poem started
A single line ago,
It will be a long one
But how long I don't know.

PLAY DAZE

If you need some time to play
You should take a holiday
There are:

Birthdays, Sabbath Days, Diwali Days and Hero
      Days, Solstice
Days, Isis Days, Bodhi Days and Garvey Days, Sun
      Days, Moon
Days, Mahavir Jayanti Days, Burns's Night Days,
      Christ Mass Days
and days called Holi Days.

Or

Whit Sundays, Orange Days, Good Fridays and
      Eid Days, Gahambar
Days, Mothers Days, Fathers Days with Boxing
      Days, Adonia Days,
Shrove Tuesdays and Tang-no-Seku Days, Easter
      Days,
Passover Days, May Days like Freedom Days.

Try

Lion of Judah Days, Chin Yeung and Tin Hau
      Days, Vaishkhi Days,
Wedding Days, Kut and Ramadan Days, New Year
      Days, Geshi Days,

Kathina and Rice Days, Hay Days, so many days to
   really get you in a daze.

When you've had your holidays
You should try a work day.

BIRTHDAYS **EVERYBODY** • SABBATH **JEWISH** • DIWALI **HINDU**
HEROES DAYS **EVERYWHERE** • SOLSTICE **PAGAN** • ISIS **ANCIENT EGYPT**
BODHI **BUDDHIST** • GARVEY **RASTAFARIAN** • SUN DAYS **TRADITIONAL**
MOON DAYS **TRADITIONAL** • MAHAVIR JAYANTI **JAIN**
BURNS'S NIGHT **SCOTTISH TRADITION** • CHRISTMAS **CHRISTIAN**
HOLI **HINDU** • WHIT SUNDAY **CHRISTIAN** • ORANGE **CHRISTIAN**
GOOD FRIDAY **CHRISTIAN** • EID **MUSLIM** • GAHAMBAR **ZOROASTRIAN**
MOTHERS DAY **TRADITIONAL** • FATHERS DAY **TRADITIONAL**
BOXING DAY **CHRISTIAN** • ADONIA **ANCIENT GREEK**
SHROVE TUESDAY **CHRISTIAN** • TANG-NO-SEKU **JAPANESE TRADITION**
EASTER **CHRISTIAN** • PASSOVER **JEWISH** • MAY DAY **WORKERS / INTERNATIONAL**
FREEDOM DAY **POLITICAL/ INTERNATIONAL** • LION OF JUDAH **RASTAFARIAN**
CHIN YEUNG **BUDDHIST** • TIN HAU **BUDDHIST** • VAISHKHI **SIKH**
WEDDING DAY **EVERYWHERE** • KUT **KOREAN** • RAMADAN **MUSLIM**
NEW YEAR **EVERYWHERE** • GESHI **JAPANESE** • KATHINA **BUDDHIST**
RICE **AFRICAN-CARIBBEAN/ASIAN TRADITIONAL**
HAY **AFRICAN-CARIBBEAN/ASIAN TRADITIONAL** • WORK DAY **EVERY DAY/EVERYWHERE**

THOUGHT FOR MONDAY

✳ **Why** do people
Complain about Mondays,
Why do
People have
Monday morning blues
And that Monday morning feeling.
Monday is like any other day.

✿ **I** think
People who suffer Monday morning blues
Read too many Sunday papers.

NOBODY DE GREAT

✗ **Nobody** is king of de jungle
Nobody rules over de sea,
Nobody is great
Nobody's my mate,
Cause dere ain't nobody
But me.

DE RONG SONG

Your house is

Falling down

Around

Your

Feet,

And you got

Nought

To eat,

Don't worry

Be happy.

Your fish

Have drowned

You wear

A frown,

You search

But you don't

Own a pound,

Don't worry

Be happy.

You ain't got

Nowhere to

Play,

Just balconies

And

Motorways,

Don't

worry

Be happy.

You meet

Someone

You really like,

They tell you to

Get on your bike,

Don't worry

Be happy.

You're on your bike

And all is fine,

You get caught

In a washing line,

Don't worry

Be happy.

You go to

school

The school is

Gone,

The Government

Put pressure on,

Don't worry

Be happy.

Your tea is
Dry
Your ice is
Hot,
Your head is
Tied up in a
Not,
Don't worry
Be happy.

You worry
Because
You're hurrying,
And hurry
Because
You're worrying,
Don't happy
Be worried.

ONLY ME

£ **Me** I am the oldest
On a young lad's quest
I am the worst at everything
And I am the best,
Yes I am the richest
I am very poor
I only need a little
But I must get some more.

✓ **My** lifespan is the longest
Really it is short
I fought so hard for freedom
And now I have been caught,
I think I own this planet
I think that I am strong
I have to drop this habit
Of never being wrong.

= **I** am the kind of teacher
Who has much to learn
The straight forward leader
Who has got to turn,
Call me Mr. President
Or call me the people,
The tutor or the student,
Because I am more equal.

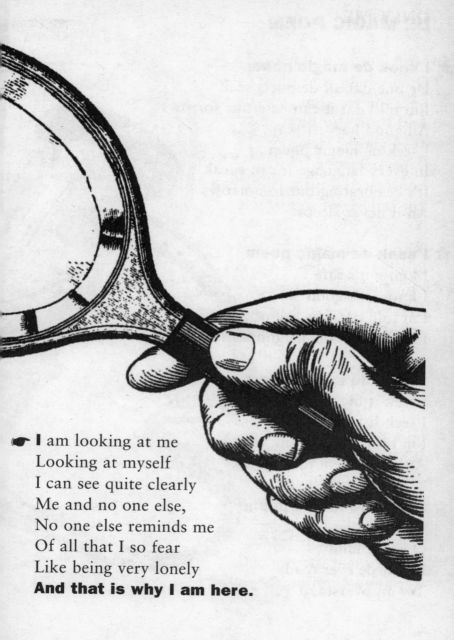

☛ I am looking at me
Looking at myself
I can see quite clearly
Me and no one else,
No one else reminds me
Of all that I so fear
Like being very lonely
And that is why I am here.

DE MAGIC POEM

★ **I seek de magic poem**
De one dat all de poets seek
I'm told dat it can ease our sorrows
An good harvest reap.
I seek de magic poem
In every language it can speak
It's celebrating our tomorrows
An it never sleeps.

☆ **I seek de magic poem**
I know it's safe
I know it's good
I'm told dat it is full of light
I need it for me neighbourhood.

☆ **I seek de magic poem**
I seek it high
I seek it low,
I'm told dat it is out of sight
Another poem told me so.

☆ **I seek de magic poem**
Over de seas
Over de land
I'm at de ever ready
Try an overstand.

☆ I seek de magic poem

It's in de mind
It's in de skies
I don't want to get heavy but
Dis poem never lies.

☆ I seek de magic poem

De one de Pop Stars cannot sing
I'm told it will bring us music
A peace place create,
I seek de magic poem
Dat poem keeps me wondering
I'm told it's pure, true an organic
Dis hide an seek is great.

GOOD COMPANY

De Queen haz a poet
I think he's very odd,
De Priest haz a poet
I think his poet's God.
De Singer haz a poet
To help de singer sing,
And de Poet haz a poet
To keep him poeting.

THIS ORANGE TREE

✿ I touched my first rose
Under this orange tree,
I was young and fruity
The sweet rose was blooming.

✝ I found faith
Under this orange tree
It was here all the time,
One day I picked it up
Then I realized
How great you are.

❧ It was under this
Very orange tree
That I read
My first Martin Luther King speech.
How great the word.

♪ It was here
Under this very orange tree,
On this very peace of earth
That I first sang
With a hummingbird.
How great the song.

♥ This orange tree knows me,
It is my friend,
I trust it and
It taste good.

IF YU SMELL

* **If yu smell** a smell
Dat makes your nostrils swell,
Be thankful dat yu have a nose at all,
An if yu cannot tell
When your flowers are unwell,
Your nose may be a little bit too small.

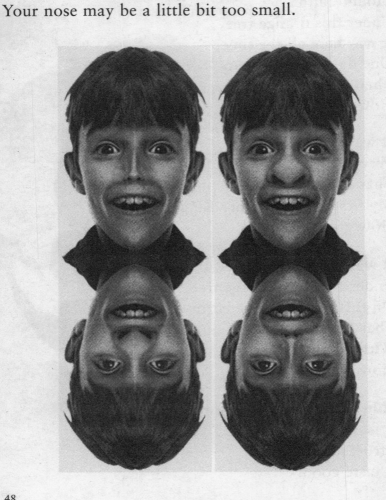

IF YU TASTE

If yu taste your lips
Let me give yu a tip,
De bottom one tastes different from de top,
An if yu taste parsnips
Dat taste a bit like chips
I think yu should return dem to de shop.

IF YU TOUCH

☞ **If yu touch** me front
I'll have to touch yu back,
An if yu touch me feet I will giggle,
Sometimes I may grunt
Like a touchy maniac
If yu touch me belly in de middle.

U.N. (UNITED NEIGHBOURS)

☛ **Me** is a simple Jamaican man
From Jamaica in de Caribbean
Me look like an African
Because Africa is me Motherlan.

☞ **Me** neighbour is a European
Born an bred in Engerlan
An we juss cannot understan
Why nations cannot live as wan.

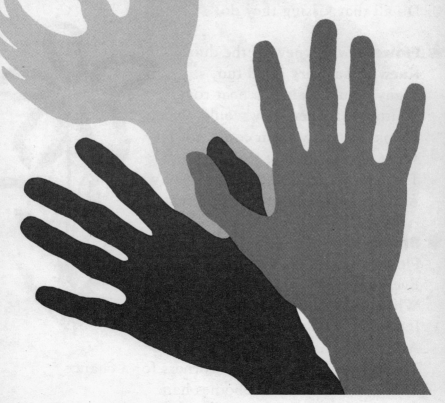

KISS AND SMELL

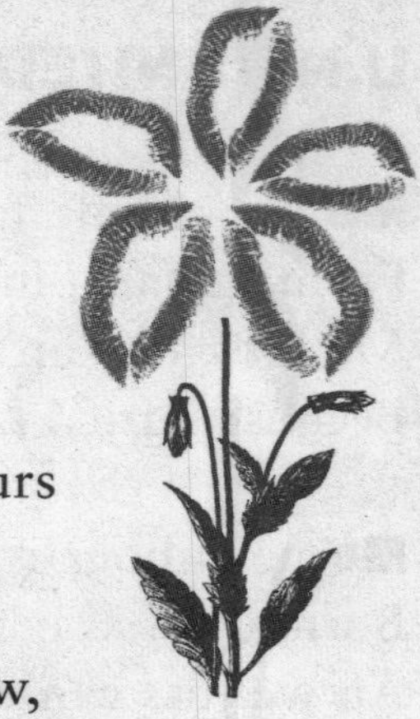

❃ **So** and so loved kissing flowers
Small ones and ones fully grown,
Sometimes they kissed them for hours
They could not leave them alone,
Their favourite places were gardens
Or big parks where big flowers grew,
They would go looking for plants then
Do all that kissing they do.

❀ **Flowers** who knew of the duo
Knew it was very good fun,
Many would wait in a neat row
Waiting for when they would come,
People who saw them could not tell
What all this kissing stuff meant,
The doctors report said they seem well
And it's lawful to sniff with intent.

❃ **Spring** times and summers were just great
Flowers would grow a big smile
Everything grew at a fast rate
When rains came to help out the soil,
Indoors they always kiss pot plants
And if they had any time spare,
They would wait on street corners for a chance
To kiss flowers in somebodies hair.

* **So** and so loved kissing flowers
Any shape, colour or size
They said 'All flowers are ours'
And 'We are for flowers'
That's wise,
So and so keep kissing flowers
Some say they may have kissed fern,
And maybe I've gone a bit sour
Waiting so long for my turn.

NO REASON, NO RHYME

➤ **A** smart poem called Limerick
Waz trying to rhyme very quick
She went berserk
When her rhyme didn't work
And now she is quite
Unwell.

HEALTH CARE

→ **All** yu Presidents
Think of de residents,
Queens an Kings
Start sharing,
City planners
Hav sum manners,
Prime ministers please
Think of de trees.

✚ **Those** dat sail
Tek care of de whales,
De strong should seek
To strengthen de weak,
Lovers of art
Should play their part,
An all those upon it
Tek care of de planet.

ALL YOU SEA

❸ Three billion gallons
Of sewage
Floating in de sea.
Whales an dolphins
Don't like it,
Seaweed an fish
Don't like it,
De dead at sea
Don't like it,
Zephaniah
Don't like it.

Three billion gallons
Of sewage
Floating in de sea.
There's a time bomb
In our water,
De boats are
Dirty too,
Three billion gallons
Of sewage,
All for you.

DOWN TO EARTH

✳ **You** gotta be cool
To live on the sun
It's pure central heating up there,
With no swimming pool
You'll bake like a bun
And fire will burn off your hair.

☆ **There** are no cars
Or bikes upon Mars
And there is still nothing to breathe,
There's no superstars
Playing guitars
And it is not easy to leave.

The moon is not **cheese** ✗
The moon is not cake
I know it's a wonderful sight,
Up there if you sneeze
Or loud noises make
They'll simply get lost in the night.

Skywards I **stare** ♟
To see what is there
Some say that I am wasting my time,
Well I must declare
I can't see no air
But I see a very good rhyme.

DEREK IN HEAVEN

✝ **Derek** in heaven
Swallowed a poem
That little poem
Just kept on growing,
Derek grew bigger
Until she was big
Then Derek the beetle
Turned into a pig.
This pig could fly
Well that's what I heard
Then our heavenly piggy
Turned into a bird,
Bird brainy Derek
Loved flying around
In this animal heaven
Where poems are found.
What's more amazing
Is that in her youth
Bird brainy Derek
Turned into a fruit,
Derek got ripe
Derek stood proud
And this juicy fruity
Would shout very loud,
This musical fruit
Had a wonderful habit
Of rapping

So then she turned into a rabbit,
One day she went into
God's great big hat
And what did she do,
She turned into a rat.
This cool rat rapper
Had the eyes of an eagle
One day as she rapped
She turned into a beetle,
Then Derek the beetle
Found heaven's big tree,
There she thrives on a diet
Of pure poetry.

GOOD HOPE

☝ **I believe**
There is enough food
On this planet
For everyone.

✌ **I believe**
That it is possible
For all people
To live in peace.

☆ **I believe**
We can live
Without guns,
I believe everyone
Is important.

✝ **I believe** there are good Christians
And good Muslims,
Good Jews
And good not sures,
I believe
There is good in everyone
I believe in people.

☙ **If I did not believe**
I would stop writing.

I know
Every day
Children cry for water,
And every day
Racists attack,
Still every day
Children play
With no care for colour.

So I believe **there is hope**
And I hope
That there are many believers
Believing
There is hope,
That is what I hope
And this is what I believe,
I believe in you,
Believe me.

DANNY LIVES ON

Danny the cat
Died last week
Killed by kicks
Of human feet,
I am sorry to say
He passed away,
A houseful of tears
I cried that day.
Danny's not with me any more
Human beings beat him
I don't know what for,
I know that some animals
Kill others to eat
But this gang just wanted to
Fight on the streets.

Danny my friend
Waz walking home
Not making trouble
And all on his own,
A few neighbours told me
That Danny then ran
And a human being kick him
To prove he's a man,
But what kind of man
Could this wicked be
I think he's a coward
He couldn't fight me.

What kind of world do we live in today,
When our future adults
Treat life this way.

Dear **Reader,**
Excuse me,
I am hurting inside,
I just don't think that we
Are near civilized,
We know how to fly
And we sail on the sea
But we don't understand
That life is a tree,
And Danny my friend
If this message gets through
You'll know this poet
Is thinking of you,
These animal beaters
Are so filled with hate,
Us animal lovers
Know Danny waz great.

SOMETHING TO WORRY ABOUT

Nothing rhymes wid **nothing**
I discovered dat today
Now I hav two more words
To help me rhyme away,
Nothing + **nothing** = **nothing**
I am good at maths as well
I feel like a professor
As me head begins to swell.

If I start wid **nothing**
I hav **nothing** to lose
And now dat I hav two **nothings**
It's easier to choose,
Nothing gets me worried
I hope you overstand
I am now enjoying **nothing**
And I hav **nothing** planned.

I am busy doing **nothing**
Me parents think it's great
I am in luv wid **nothing**
And there's **nothing** dat I hate,
I will give you **nothing**
So you hav **nothing** to fear
Let me tell you **nothing**
I hav **nothing** to declare.

Nothing's rong wid **nothing**
It's such a great idea
It need not be created
I hav **nothing** to share,
Nothing rhymes wid **nothing**
There waz **nothing** at de start
And I can't give you anything
When there's **nothing** in my heart.

GOING LOTTO

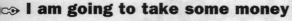

I think I've won the lottery
My goodness me I am rich
Now I'll throw away my clothes
And replace every stitch,
I think I've won the lottery
I am going to buy some fame
I am going to buy my own police
Who will protect my name.

I am going to take some money
And buy myself a plane
And when I've been around the world
I'll just go round again,
I am going to take some money
And buy some quietness
I am going to buy a doctor
Who can get rid of my stress.

I am going to buy me every zoo
And let the animals out
Then I'll get my quietness
And really, really shout,
I'll do just what I want to
With all that money of mine
And if I get too busy
I'll buy myself some time.

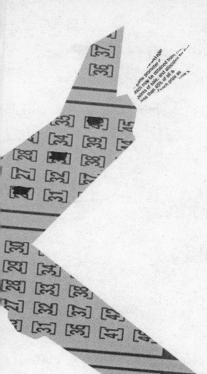

I think I've won the lottery ✧⊷

I think, I think, I think
I think
Therefore
I think I'll buy myself
The missing link,
And if I've won the lottery
I'll buy lots of goodbyes
Then I will give them happily
To all the racist guys.

I think I've won the lottery ✐

My goodness greatness me
I must get some security
And protect my prize money,
But don't go telling everybody
Think before you speak
I get this feeling regularly
I thought the same last week.

FAIR DEAL

❀ Rick de rapper
Met a shopper
At de May Day fair,
Said Rick de rapper
To de shopper,
'What are you doing here?'
De shopper said,
'I come to buy a Helter Skelter Rick,
I've got a bit of money
And I've got to spend it quick!'

● Rick de rapper said,
'Look shopper,
Let's be sensible,
You cannot buy that Helter Skelter
It's unbuyable.'
De shopper started crying
He was a saddened chap,
But it was not for buying
Rick de rapper
Told him dat.

✚ They met one hour later,
By the First Aid shelter,
De shopper told de rapper
Dat he owns de Helter Skelter,
Rick said,
'I am sure you can't buy

Helter Skelters here.'
De shopper said,
'Us millionaires
Just simply buy the fair.'

WALKING BLACK HOME

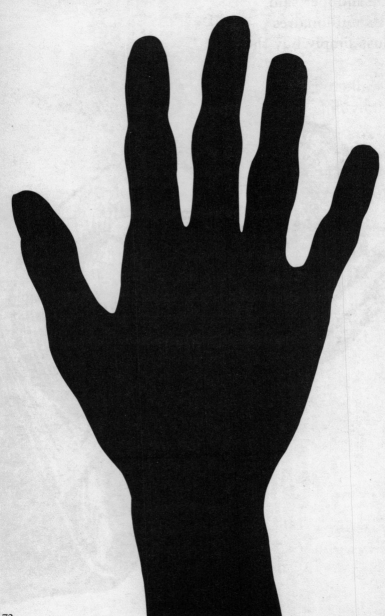

♠ **That** day waz
A bad day,

I walked for
Many miles,

Unlike me,
I did not

Return any
Smiles.

Tired,

Weak
And
Hungry,

But I
Would not
Turn

Back,

Sometimes it's hard
To get a taxi
When you're **Black**.

PROTEST POETS

Dem sey
Dere is now
A computer
Dat writes poems,
Or to put it another way,
A computer
Dat's a poet.

How does it relax?
Wot's its inspiration?
An does it sign autographs?
Does it wake up
In de middle of de night
An sey,
'I've got a great idea,
Where's me floppy disk?'
Or is it one of those poets
Dat don't say much.

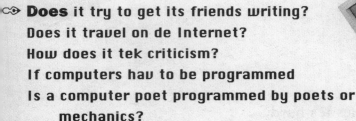

Does it try to get its friends writing?
Does it travel on de Internet?
How does it tek criticism?
If computers hav to be programmed
Is a computer poet programmed by poets or
    mechanics?
How does such a poet perform poems,
An do dey perform to people
Or computers?

Is dere a factory somewhere
Full of poets in white coats
Wid screwdrivers an microchips in their pockets?

♥ **These** are de questions
Dat every decent human poet should ask,
We human poets should unite
Lest we pass on to future poets
A world in which
Poets do not fall in love
Or mek mistakes
An all inspiration is programmed,

☞ **WE DEMAND A FUTURE**
Where poets do silly things,
Like
Sleep in socks,
Wear flares,
An talk to caterpillars,
A future where poets
Scratch,
Wonder,
An cry on de page.

DOUBLE TALK

Not, not, not, not
A lot, a lot, a lot, a lot
Of, of, of, of
People, people, people, people
Know, know, know, know
Dat, dat, dat, dat
Dis, dis, dis, dis
Page, page, page, page
Has, has, has, has
A great, a great, a great, a great
Echo, echo, echo, echo, echo, echo, echo,
echo, echo, echo.

Not, not, not, not
A lot, a lot, a lot, a lot
Of, of, of, of
People, people, people, people
Know, know, know, know
Dat, dat, dat, dat
Dis, dis, dis, dis
Page, page, page, page
Has, has, has, has
A great, a great, a great, a great
Echo, echo, echo, echo, echo, echo, echo, ec

Double Talk

Not, not, not, not

A lot, a lot, a

Of, of, of, of

People, people, people,

Know, know, know, kno

Dat, dat, dat, dat

Dis, dis, dis, dis

Page, page, page, page

Has, has, has, has

A great, a great, a g

Echo, echo, echo, echo,

echo, echo.

FOOTBALL MAD

Oh no, bless my soul
Clever Trevor's scored a goal.

So he runs up the pitch
And wriggles his botty,
He is kissed by ten men
All sweaty and snotty,
Now he's waving his fist
To the Queen who just stares
The lad's going crazy
But everyone cheers.
Now what's he doing?
He's chewing the cud!
Now what's he doing?
He's rolling in mud!
Now he is crying
I think he's in pain
Now what's he doing?
He's smiling again.

On no, bless my soul
Clever Trevor's scored a goal.

✝ He's doing gymnastics

He's doing some mime
He's kissing the ground
For a very long time,
He's now on his back
With his feet in the air
Now he's gone all religious
And stopped for a prayer.
Did he pray for the sick?
Did he pray for the poor?
No, he prayed for the ball
And he prayed to score.
No one but no one
Can re-start the game
Until Trevor has had
His moment of fame.

☞ Oh no, bless my soul

Clever Trevor's scored a goal,
He kicked the ball into the net
How much money will he get?

BIG BABY

Once I was a twinkle
In my father's eye,
Once I was my mother's
Dream come true,
Now I am a hippy
Rappy Rasta guy
Trying to invent
A rhyme or two.

Once I was a
Smelly little baby,
Once I was kissed
Every single day,
Now everybody thinks
That I am crazy
As I dilly dally dolly
On my way.

HOME ALONE

✎ **Mum's got a telly** of her own
Dad's got a telly of his own
Baby got a telly of his own
Little sister got a telly of her own.

✎ **Cat got a telly** of her own
Mouse got a telly of his own
I got a telly of my own
To make me feel at home.

HIP-HOP COP

He looks a bit like
Fred Astaire
He's off on tour
Everywhere,
He can't stop
He luvs to rock,
He's de hip-hop cop
From de big cop shop.

Dressed in blue
He funky chickens
He danced right through
Me vegan kitchen,
Dancing is his favourite sport
I've even seen him dance in court.

He's de hip-hop cop
From de big cop shop,
Always there
An liked a lot,
Me mom thinks he's really sweet
He is always on
De beat,
He's de hip-hop cop
From de big cop shop,
A criminal
He never got,
But he got riddim

He got soul
An he is
Fifty-five years old.

He raps in **his**
Walkie talkie
To a copper
In Milwaukee,
Once he caught
Discomania
On a dance floor
In Romania,
Now de hip-hop cop
Is doing fine
His body's always
Doing time,
Never keen to
Make arrest
But always keen
To dance his best.

When de hip-hop **cop**
Is in our town
There is no crime
We all get down,
To de wicked beat
Wid our wicked feet
An it's very safe
To walk de streets,

When de hip-hop cop
Is in fine style
Michael Jackson
Runs a mile
An folk like me
Shout hip-hooray,
Why can't all coppers
Dance dis way.

He's de hip-hop cop
From de big cop shop
Always there
An liked a lot
He lays down
De groovy law
An he
Really
Knows de score,
He's de hip-hop cop
From de big cop shop
He seems to dance
Wid ease
Non-stop,
No one's ever seen
Him stumble,
In dis urban
Concrete jungle.

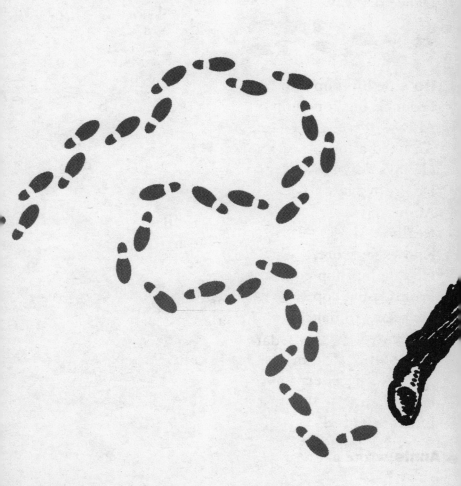

WRITE A WAY

✍ Benny

w e a
r t
o o e
p m
d
a
t
b
e
n
d
s,
s
d
n
e
c
s
a
dat
m
e
o
p

✍ Annie wrote a

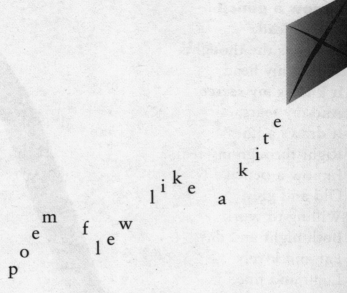

        p o e m   f l e w   l i k e   a   k i t e

✎ **Kitty's**

•◦ **And Penny** wrote a poem dat writes. ☞

PENCIL ME IN

 I know a pencil
Full of lead,
It knows the thoughts
Within my head,
It knows my secrets
And my fears,
It draws a line
Right through my tears.
I know a pencil
Old and grey,
Willing to work
Both night and day,
Fat and lovely
Light and fine,
It moves with me
Through space and time.

 Be they good
Or be they bad,
It tells of all
The dreams I have,
And when I have
No oar to row,
It writes a way
And lets me go.
When baby words
Are crying loud,
It touches words

And makes me proud,
A work of art
It is no fake,
It really has
A point to make.

This pencil sees
The best of me,
The worst
And all the rest
Of me,
And as I go
Through puberty,
It changes all my
Poetry.
It goes with me
On all my tours,
It fought with me
In all word wars,
And peacefully
This pencil tries
To help me learn
And make me wise.

Every pencil needs a hand
And every mind needs to expand,
I know a pencil,
What you see
Is me and it
In harmony.

89

FUNKY CHICKEN

A funky chicken ate my corn
But really I don't mind,
My funky friend eats my dinner
Every time I dine,
He said that he's a big fan
Of my rhyming poetry,
So when we get together
We double talk turkey.

Gobble, gobble

A funky chicken nicked my pants
But I think that's OK,
I'm the kind of rhymer
That wears two pairs anyway,
Yesterday he nicked my lemon flavoured socks,
And the last time that I saw him
He was growing dreadlocks.

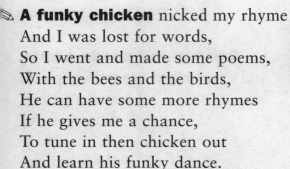

A funky chicken nicked my rhyme
And I was lost for words,
So I went and made some poems,
With the bees and the birds,
He can have some more rhymes
If he gives me a chance,
To tune in then chicken out
And learn his funky dance.

✓ **A funky chicken** spent my cash
I'm broke but I don't care,
This chicken has so much style
The chicks just stand and stare,
Human beings are unaware
Of all the fun they're missing,
Until they see this very funky chicken
Funky Chicken.

This feathery funky flapper
Is really flipping great,
He's the pick of the pops with the pecker
And I'm proud that he's my mate,
When he nicked my music
I told him not to stop,
One day I'll introduce him to
That friendly hip-hop cop.

INDEX OF FIRST LINES